SHADOWS OF SILENCE: Whispers In the Chapel.

By

Bibian N Okoye

Copyright©2024 Bibian N Okoye

Legal Notice:

Disclaimer:

The information provided in this book is for educational and informational purposes only and is not intended as a substitute for professional advice, diagnosis, or treatment. The content is based on the author's research and personal experiences and should not be considered as a comprehensive resource. Readers are encouraged to consult with qualified professionals regarding any specific concerns or questions related to their situation, particularly regarding mental health, parenting, or related issues.

The author and publisher disclaim any liability or responsibility for any loss or damage, including but not limited to indirect or consequential loss or damage, arising from reliance on any information provided in this book. The views and opinions expressed in this book are solely those of the author and do not necessarily reflect the official policy or position of any affiliated organizations.

DEDICATION

To Aunty Caroline,

Whose silent strength and untold suffering shaped the legacy of our family.

In your shadowed journey, we find echoes of resilience, faith, and an enduring light.

This is for those who, like you, carry their burdens in silence—

May your story speak for the voiceless, and may your memory remind us that even in the darkest corners of life, grace and hope can still emerge.

May these whispers in the chapel offer solace to every soul seeking redemption.

FOREWORD

In every family's history, there are stories whispered rather than spoken, buried beneath layers of tradition, silence, and sometimes shame. Shadows of Silence: Whispers in the Chapel delves into one such narrative—the haunting tale of Aunty Caroline. A figure whose life was marked by resilience, sorrow, and an enduring faith tested by unspeakable tragedy.

This book does not just chronicle Caroline's story; it is a tribute to the silent strength of women who have borne the weight of secrets, yet remained unbroken. Within the sacred space of the chapel, where prayers once floated heavenward, Caroline found both her sanctuary and the source of her deepest pain. Violated in the very house of God, she carried her burden quietly, her suffering witnessed by stone walls that could neither confess nor console. The violation altered the course of her life, leading to her rejection by those she trusted most, and casting a long shadow over her existence.

And yet, even in the face of relentless sorrow, Caroline became a symbol of endurance. Her choice to remain solitary, to forego marriage and the comforts of societal acceptance, reflected a quiet defiance. She bore her pain, her love, and her tragedy, and through it all, her story lives on—passed down through her family like an heirloom.

This tale of heartbreak and resilience challenges us to confront the darker realities that often reside in the quiet corners of our communities. It calls us to listen to the echoes of the past, to bear witness to those whose stories were silenced, and to find compassion where once there was condemnation.

As you turn these pages, may Caroline's whispered legacy speak to you. May her strength inspire empathy, and may her light shine—offering hope even in life's darkest moments.

Let her story be a reminder: no silence, however heavy, can last forever.

— BIBIAN OKOYE

Author, and Storyteller

TABLE OF CONTENT

INTRODUCTION

A subtle nod to the sacred space where Caroline story unfolds.

In the quiet corners of our family's history, there exists a tale of sorrow and resilience. It begins with a young woman named Aunty Caroline; her spirit once radiant like the morning sun. She served faithfully in the dimly lit chapel, her prayers echoing through the stone walls.

But darkness crept into her life—a shadow that would forever alter her path. A man, face obscured by sin, violated her innocence. The secret she carried weighed heavily upon her soul, a burden too heavy for confession.

The priest, a stern figure with eyes that pierced the veil of secrets, sensed her anguish. His gaze bore into her, unravelling threads of guilt and shame. When he discovered her truth, his wrath was swift. He cursed her, condemning her to a life of desolation.

She chose solitude over marriage, her womb a vessel for both love and tragedy. She gave birth to a child, a son, born from pain and sorrow. His fragile life was a testament to her endurance, but he too was taken by the cruel hand of fate.

And so, she became a silent monument—a testament to endurance, a beacon of sorrow.

In the small village of Iruowelle Igboukwu in a suburb area of a country called Nigeria, where the chapel's stone walls held secrets as ancient as time, there lived a young woman named Caroline. Her presence was a beacon—a light that guided weary souls towards hope.

Caroline's days were filled with devotion. She swept the chapel floor, polished the tarnished candlesticks, and whispered prayers that echoed through the dimly lit space. Her faith was unwavering, her heart pure.

But shadows have a way of creeping into even the holiest of places. One moonless night, as Caroline knelt in prayer, a man entered. His face obscured by darkness; he violated her innocence. The chapel's sacred silence bore witness to her pain.

Caroline carried her secret like a heavy stone, unable to confess to the priest she served. His stern eyes seemed to pierce her very soul, yet he remained unaware of her torment.

When the priest finally discovered her truth, his wrath was swift. He cursed her—a curse that clung to her like a shroud. Caroline chose solitude over marriage, her womb becoming a vessel for both love and tragedy.

And so, Caroline became a silent monument—a testament to endurance, a beacon of sorrow.

May Caroline story find its voice through my words and may her light shine even in the darkest of moments!!!

CHAPTER ONE

The Violation

The chapel's stone walls held secrets—whispers of prayers, echoes of devotion. Caroline knelt there, her heart a fragile vessel, when darkness slithered in.

He came—a man with a face veiled by sin. His touch defiled her innocence, leaving scars unseen. Caroline's silent screams echoed through the sacred space, but the chapel remained indifferent.

The secret she carried weighed upon her soul, a burden too heavy for confession. She scrubbed the floors, polished the candlesticks, and wondered if God heard her cries.

The priest, stern and unyielding, never suspected. His gaze bore into her, unravelling threads of guilt and shame. But he remained blind to the shadows that clung to her.

And so, Caroline became a prisoner of silence—a victim of the chapel's hallowed walls.

Caroline's pain reverberated through the chapel's cold stones, a silent cry that echoed beyond the stained-glass windows. Her parents, once pillars of strength, turned away, unable to bear the weight of her shame. Siblings whispered behind closed doors; their voices hushed but their judgment sharp.

In the quiet hours, Caroline clung to her faith—the only solace left. But even God seemed distant, His presence obscured by the veil of her violation. She wondered if redemption were possible if forgiveness could mend the fractured pieces of her soul.

The mighty had indeed fallen—the radiant light dimmed to a flicker. Caroline's steps grew heavier, her shoulders bowed beneath the burden of secrecy. She became a ghost within her own family, a shadow moving silently through the rooms where laughter once danced.

And still, the shame lingered—a relentless companion. Caroline's tears baptized the chapel floor, each drop a plea for release. But the walls held their secrets, and her voice remained trapped within them.

In the hallowed silence, Caroline's story awaited its teller—a witness who would finally break the chains of shame and let her agony breathe..

CHAPTER TWO

The Priest's Revelation

The chapel's stone walls held more than echoes of prayers—they concealed secrets that gnawed at Caroline's soul. The priest, stern and unyielding, moved through the dimly lit space like a shadow. His eyes, sharp as the blade of a sacrificial knife, missed nothing.

One day, as Caroline knelt in penance, the priest approached. His gaze bore into her, unravelling threads of guilt and shame. She trembled, fearing he had glimpsed her hidden truth—the violation that stained her innocence.

But the priest's revelation was not what she expected. He spoke in hushed tones, his voice a whisper carried by the chapel's sacred silence. "Caroline," he said, "I see your burden. Your secret is known to me."

She gasped, her heart pounding. Had he come to condemn her further? To amplify her shame? Instead, he continued, "You are not alone. There are others who have not bowed down before Baal, whose mouths have never kissed his idol."

Caroline's tears flowed freely. Seven thousand souls, hidden like stars behind storm clouds, shared her defiance. The priest's curse had not silenced them all.

And so, in that quiet moment, Caroline glimpsed redemption—a fragile hope that perhaps her suffering was not in vain.

Caroline's burden weighed heavily upon her, etching lines of sorrow into her face. The priest's pronouncement echoed through the village, casting a shadow over her family. Whispers spread like wildfire— words not of compassion, but of judgment.

Yet, in the quiet of her room, Caroline clung to hope. The Creator knew her secret—the pain etched into her very bones. She carried the baby, each kick a reminder of both sin and survival. When the time came, she laboured alone, her tears mingling with the sweat of childbirth.

The child—a son—was named Cyprian. His tiny fingers grasped hers, a fragile connection to a world that had betrayed her. But Cyprian's breath was fleeting, like a candle snuffed out by the wind.

The family hushed their voices, but the story remained— a whispered legacy of shame and regret. The brothers' children, born long after Caroline's passing, carried the weight of her sacrifice. They knew the truth—the light that had dimmed, the church abandoned.

In the quiet of their own hearts, they wondered: Could forgiveness ever pierce the shadows? Could redemption bloom from the soil of silence?

And so, the chapel stood empty, its pews gathering dust. Caroline's faith had crumbled, replaced by idols—their faces cold, their promises hollow. But somewhere, in the hidden corners of memory, her story lingered—a plea for understanding, a cry for mercy.

May we, too, remember Caroline—the silent monument—and find compassion where others found condemnation.

CHAPTER THREE

Solitude and Sacrifice

Caroline's solitude became her sanctuary—a refuge from the judgmental whispers that swirled like autumn leaves. She retreated to the chapel, its stone walls absorbing her tears. The altar, once a place of devotion, now bore witness to her sacrifice.

Caroline's world had crumbled, her innocence stolen, and her spirit burdened by a secret too heavy to bear. The priest's harsh judgment and the community's whispers left her isolated, a solitary figure in a world that had turned its back on her.

The Weight of Solitude

Caroline chose solitude over marriage, a decision that set her apart from the expectations of her time. She retreated into the quiet corners of her home and the chapel, seeking solace in the familiar rituals of her faith. The chapel, once a place of communal worship, became her sanctuary—a space where she could confront her pain without fear of judgment.

In the stillness of her solitude, Caroline found a strange kind of strength. She embraced the silence, allowing it to envelop her like a comforting shroud. Her prayers, once whispered in the company of others, now became intimate conversations with God. She poured out her heart, seeking understanding and forgiveness.

The Birth of a Child

She refused marriage, her womb a sacred vessel that held both love and tragedy

The children she carried were testament— fragile lives born from pain.

Caroline's solitude was interrupted by the birth of her child—a son born from the violence she had endured. She named him Cyprian, a name that carried the weight of both love and sorrow. Cyprian's arrival was a bittersweet moment, a reminder of the pain she had suffered but also a testament to her resilience.

Caroline's love for Cyprian was fierce and unwavering. She cradled him in her arms, singing lullabies that echoed through the empty rooms of her home. But Cyprian's life was fragile, and he was taken from her too soon. His death left a void that no amount of prayer could fill.

He slipped away like sand through her fingers. Caroline's family turned away, their eyes avoiding hers. But the brothers' children—the inheritors of her legacy— remembered. They whispered her story, passing it down like an heirloom. And so, the light that had dimmed cast shadows upon their hearts.

The chapel stood empty, its pews gathering dust. Caroline's faith crumbled, replaced by idols. Yet somewhere, in the hidden corners of memory, her sacrifice lingered—a plea for redemption, a cry for understanding.

In solitude, she found strength. In sacrifice, she became a silent monument.

A Life of Sacrifice

Caroline's life became a series of sacrifices. She gave up the possibility of marriage and a family of her own, choosing instead to dedicate herself to the memory of her children and the service of the chapel. Her days were filled with acts of devotion—cleaning the chapel, tending to the altar, and maintaining the sacred space.

Her sacrifices did not go unnoticed. The community, once quick to judge, began to see Caroline in a new light. Her unwavering faith and quiet strength inspired those around her. She became a symbol of resilience, a reminder that even in the face of unimaginable pain, one could find a way to endure.

The Legacy of Solitude

Caroline's story did not end with her death. Her legacy lived on through her family, who continued to honor her memory and the sacrifices she had made. Her brother Alex, inspired by her strength, brought light back into the family. He led them back to the faith, rekindling their devotion to God.

Caroline's presence was felt in the whispers of the wind, in the flicker of candlelight, and in the hearts of those who remembered her. Her story, once shrouded in silence, became a beacon of hope and resilience. Her family, determined to honor her memory, continued to tell her story, passing it down through the generations.

In the quiet of the chapel, Caroline's spirit lingered—a silent monument to her endurance and sacrifice. Her light, once dimmed, now shone brightly, illuminating the path for those who followed.

It is heartwarming to hear how brother Alex rekindled the family's faith, bringing light back into our lives. Caroline's memory lives on—a testament to her endurance and the shadows she carried. She was innocent, yet her suffering weighed heavily upon her. Our prayers honour her, and through them, a new light will indeed shine—one that transcends pain and illuminates' hope.

Let us delve into the mystical realm where imaginary beings roam—a place where the veil between reality and wonder is thin.

CHAPTER FOUR

Echoes in the Chapel

In the hollowed bones of chapel walls, ghostly whispers rise and fall. Laughter from ages past reverberates—a mournful drawl etched into the stones.

Once, hymns were sung in candle's glow. Congregation hearts swayed to ancient voices, soft and slow. These echoes linger where shadows grow.

Oh, The echoes in the chapel ruins...

Songs of old still commune in the silence. Haunting tales, winds attune.

Windows shattered, arms of vine—timeless prayers entwined in roots. Holy ghost's cross boundary lines, their presence enshrined in dust.

Bells now mute, their tolls erased. Yet in the silence, notes remain embraced. Saints and sinners lost, and displaced time has caused the ruins.

Oh, The echoes in the chapel ruins...

They whisper stories of faith and sorrow, of souls who sought solace within these walls. Their resonance transcends time, bridging the gap between the living and the departed.

May we listen closely, for within these echoes lie forgotten prayers, unspoken confessions, and the quiet resilience of those who once sought refuge here.

The chapel, once vibrant with hymns and whispered prayers, now stands as a relic of memory. Its timeworn stones cradle the echoes of countless souls who sought solace within its walls.

The Fading Organ

- The organ, its pipes tarnished, and keys worn, once thundered with devotion. Now, only a faint echo remains—a spectral melody that weaves through the rafters. Caroline's fingers once danced across those keys, her heart pouring into each note.

The Unanswered Amen

- In the quiet hours, Caroline knelt, her lips forming silent prayers. The priest's curse had silenced her confessions, but her faith endured. The chapel absorbed her whispered amens, holding them close like fragile butterflies.

The Dusty Pews

- Rows of empty pews bear witness to generations. Caroline's family, once scattered by shame, now reunites. Alex, the beacon of redemption, sits where Caroline once knelt. His children listen, their hearts open to the echoes of forgiveness.

The Stained Glass

- Sunlight filters through stained glass, casting kaleidoscopic patterns on the floor. Caroline's face, etched in coloured shards, gazes down. Her eyes—both haunted and hopeful—seem to pierce time itself.

The Whispering Breeze

- As twilight settles, a breeze slips through the broken window. It carries Caroline's story—a fragile parchment—to the heavens. Perhaps angels listen, their wings brushing against the chapel's eaves.

The Unseen Choir

• Caroline's child, his name etched in air, form an ethereal choir. His voice together with angels rise, harmonizing with the wind. Each note—a fragile thread connecting past and present.

The Final Amen

• And so, the chapel's echoes blend—a symphony of sorrow and redemption. Caroline's light, once dimmed, now flickers anew. The congregation, Alex's descendants, lift their voices. Together, they offer the final amen.

May these echoes resonate beyond the pages—a testament to Caroline's endurance, the chapel's legacy, and the fragile beauty of forgiveness.

Next Chapter: The silent monument that stands as a testament to Caroline's endurance and the weight of her story:

CHAPTER FIVE

The Silent Monument

Caroline's story did not end with her death. Her presence lingered, a whisper in the shadows, a silent guardian watching over her family. The chapel, once a place of solace and sorrow, became a conduit for her spirit, her whispers echoing through its ancient walls.

The chapel, its timeworn stones etched with memories, stands as a silent witness. Caroline's legacy—both burden and blessing—clings to its walls.

The Weathered Altar

•   Caroline knelt here; her whispered prayers absorbed by the wood. The altar, once adorned with fresh flowers, now cradles dust. Yet within its grain, her devotion lingers.

The Flickering Candle

•   A single candle, perpetually lit, casts shadows on the chapel floor. Caroline's flame—dimmed but unyielding—illuminates the darkest corners. It dances, a fragile heartbeat.

The Unread Scriptures

- Bibles rest on the wooden lectern, their pages untouched. Caroline's faith was written in her scars, not ink. Her story—the unwritten gospel—echoes through the empty pews.

The Stained-Glass Window

- Caroline's face, captured in coloured glass, gazes down. Her eyes—both haunted and hopeful—seem to pierce time itself. The sun, when it aligns, paints her features with celestial hues.

The Unheard Choir

- Caroline's child, his name whispered by unseen lips, form an ethereal choir. His voice rise, harmonizing with the wind. Each note—a fragile thread connecting past and present.

- Caroline's footsteps, imprinted on the chapel floor, lead nowhere. She walked this path—alone, burdened—her heart echoing in each step. The dust clings, refusing to forget.

The Final Amen

- And so, the chapel stands—a silent monument. Caroline's light, once dimmed, now flickers anew. The congregation, Alex's descendants, lift their voices. Together, they offer the final amen.

CHAPTER SIX

The Silent Guardian

Caroline's spirit, though unseen, was felt by those who were attuned to the whispers of the past. Her presence was a comforting shadow, a reminder that she had not truly left. She visited her family in dreams, her ethereal form a beacon of hope and resilience.

In these dreams, Caroline's message was clear: she wanted her story to be told, her innocence and royalty to be honored. Her whispers carried the weight of her pain and the strength of her spirit, urging her family to remember and to share her tale.

The Dream Visitations

One night, Caroline appeared in a dream to her niece, a young woman named Clara. In the dream, Caroline stood in the chapel, bathed in a soft, otherworldly light. Her eyes, filled with both sorrow and determination, met Clara's.

"Tell my story," Caroline whispered, her voice like the rustling of leaves. "Let the world know of my innocence and my sacrifice. Honor my memory and let my light shine once more."

Clara awoke with a start, her heart pounding. She knew that Caroline's message was not just a dream—it was a call to action. She shared the dream with her family, and together, they vowed to honor Caroline's wishes.

The Family's Resolve

Caroline's family, inspired by her whispers, began to piece together her story. They gathered in the chapel, their voices mingling with the echoes of the past. Each family member contributed a piece of the puzzle, their collective memories forming a tapestry of Caroline's life.

They spoke of her unwavering faith, her tragic violation, and the birth of her son. They remembered her strength in the face of adversity and her enduring love for her family. As they shared their stories, the chapel came alive, the whispers of the past blending with the voices of the present.

CHAPTER SEVEN

The Chapel's Echoes

The chapel, once a place of sorrow, became a sanctuary of remembrance. that would be cool this the whispers in the shadow grew louder, each echoing a testament to Caroline's enduring spirit. Her story, once shrouded in silence, now resonated through the chapel's ancient walls.

Visitors to the chapel could feel Caroline's presence. They spoke of a gentle breeze that carried her whispers, of a soft light that illuminated the darkest corners. The chapel became a place of pilgrimage, where people came to honor Caroline's memory and to find solace in her story.

The Legacy of Whispers

Caroline's whispers transcended time, reaching across generations. Her family, now united in their resolve, continued to share her story. They wrote it down, ensuring that her legacy would not be forgotten.

Caroline's light, once dimmed by tragedy, now shone brightly. Her story became a beacon of hope and resilience, inspiring others to find strength in their darkest moments. The whispers in the shadow, once a symbol of sorrow, now carried a message of redemption and love.

CHAPTER EIGHT

Epilogue: The Eternal Light

I have answered the call to tell the world that though you are gone, you are still living. Your light is shining, glowing among us, illuminating everyone in the family. You shame the enemies and promote the presence of God, whom you cherished so much and vowed to serve.

Caroline, your spirit lingers in the whispers of the wind, in the flicker of candlelight, and in the hearts of those who remember. Your story, once shrouded in silence, now finds its voice through me. I am here, inspired by your unwavering faith and resilience, to share your tale with the world.

You were a handmaid of God, a beacon of purity and devotion. Though you faced unimaginable pain and sorrow, your light never dimmed. It shines brighter now, guiding us, your family, back to the path of faith and love.

In your honor, we continue to pray, to seek forgiveness, and to cherish the love of God. Your legacy lives on, a testament to your innocence and royalty. May your story inspire others to find strength in their darkest moments and to believe in the enduring power of faith.

Caroline, your light is eternal. It glows within us, a reminder of your sacrifice and your unwavering spirit. We honor you; we remember you, and we carry your light forward, illuminating the world with your story.

May Your Soul Rest in Perfect Peace